The Stations of the Cross for Children

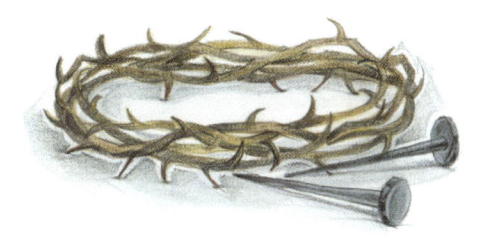

Text by Jerry Windley-Daoust

Illustrations by Vicki Shuck

peanut butter & grace

Winona, Minnesota

See page 34 for ways to use this book.

The Stations of the Cross for Children
Text copyright © 2018 by Jerry Windley-Daoust.
Art copyright © 2018 Vicki Shuck.
Book design by Jerry Windley-Daoust and Steve Nagel.
Copy editing by Karen Carter.

All rights reserved. No part of this book may be reproduced by any means without the written permission of the publisher.

Unless otherwise noted, Scripture quotations in this work are from New Revised Standard Version Bible: Catholic Edition, copyright © 1989, 1993 National Council of the Churches of Christ in the United States of America. Used by permission. All rights reserved worldwide.

Nihil obstat:
  Rev. Timothy Hall, Censor librorum
  February 7, 2018

Imprimatur:
  †Most Rev. John M. Quinn, Bishop of Winona
  February 7, 2018

First Edition: 2018
ISBN 978-1-944008-53-6
Printed in the United States of America.

peanut butter & grace

Peanut Butter & Grace Books are published by

gracewatch.media

Winona, Minnesota
www.gracewatch.media

Opening Prayer

God loved the world so much,
he sent his only Son, Jesus,
to bring the good news
of God's love and mercy to everyone.

Jesus told people this good news,
healing them and forgiving their sins.
Then he and his friends went
to share the good news in Jerusalem.

Crowds of people came out to meet him,
shouting, "Hosanna! Blessed is the king!"
This made the rulers angry.
They wanted to be in charge, not Jesus.
They decided to kill Jesus.

Let's pray.

Jesus, you loved us no matter what—
even when it meant dying on a cross.
As we remember what you did for us,
make our spirits strong,
so we can love as much as you did.

Amen.

1
The Last Supper
Matthew 26:26-29

The last time Jesus ate with his friends,
he gave them bread and wine and said,
"This is my body and blood,
which I am giving you for
the forgiveness of sins."

Let's be quiet with Jesus.

Let's pray.

Jesus, you give your whole self to us
in the Eucharist
every time we celebrate Mass.

May we thank you
for this wonderful gift
by giving our whole selves to you
in all we say and do.

Amen.

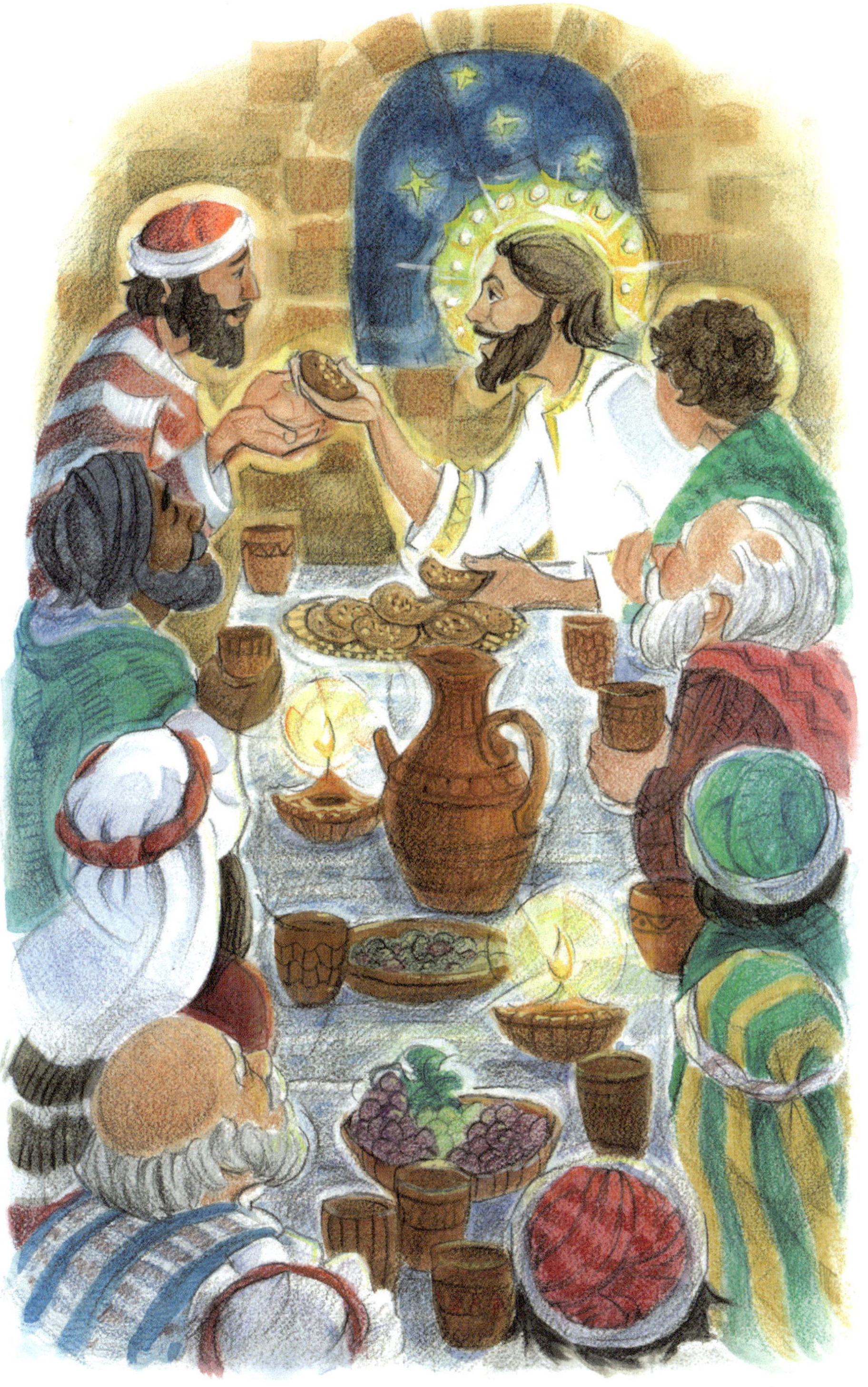

2
The agony in the garden
Luke 22:39-48

After Jesus ate with his friends,
they went to a garden.
Jesus was very sad and scared
because he knew that soon
he would suffer and die.
He asked his friends
to pray with him,
but they fell asleep.
An angel came from heaven
to give him strength.

Let's be quiet with Jesus.

Let's pray.

Jesus, we pray for
anyone who is feeling
sad or scared today.

Please send your Spirit
to comfort them and make them strong,
and help us make them feel better.

Amen.

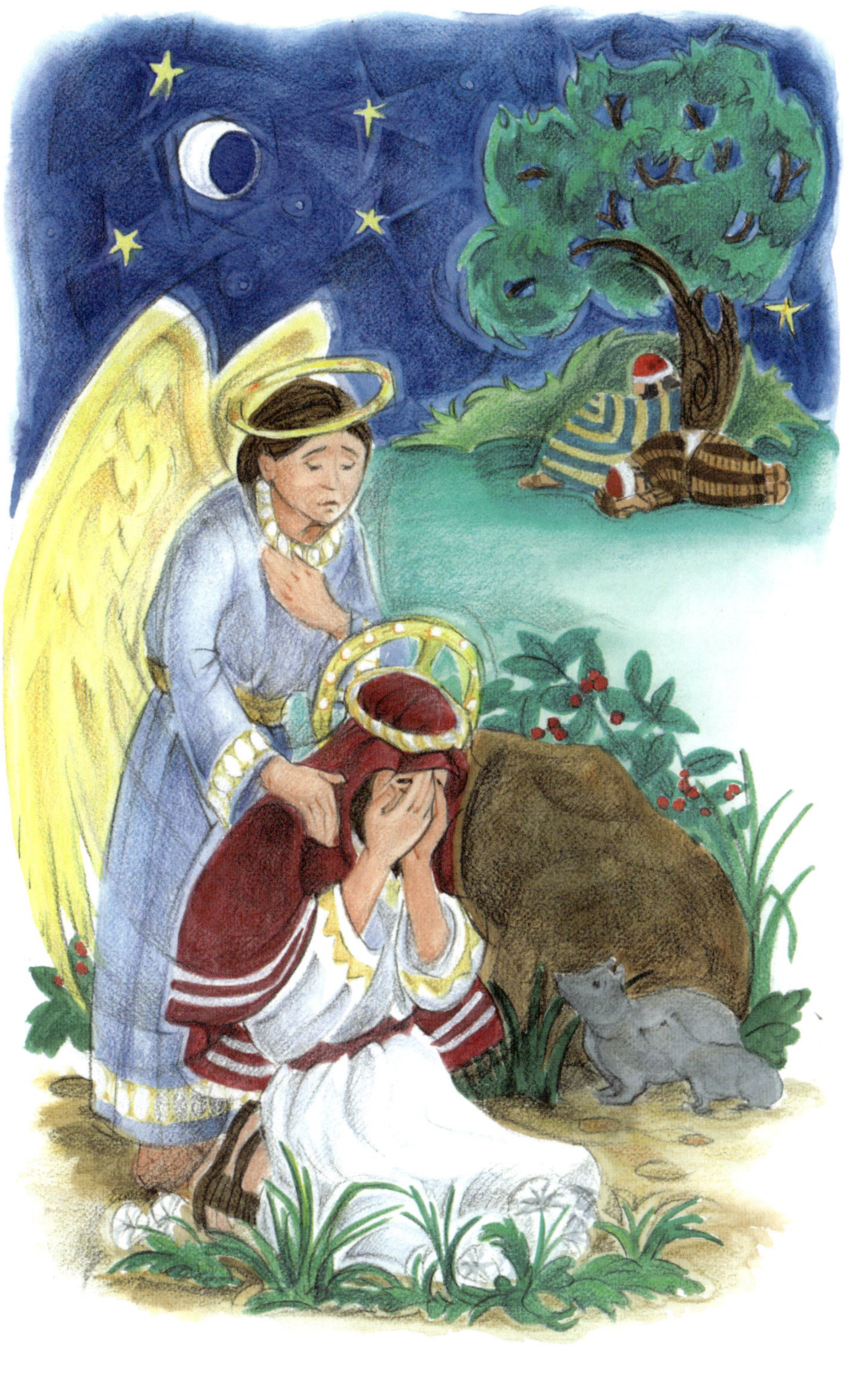

3
Jesus is condemned to death
Matthew 27:15-26

Some people came to arrest Jesus.
They took him to the governor.
They said Jesus should be killed
because he wanted to be the king.
The governor said Jesus
had not done anything wrong,
but the people shouted,
"Crucify him! Crucify him!"

Let's be quiet with Jesus.

Let's pray.

Jesus, sometimes we are like the people
who wanted to hurt you.
Sometimes we are mean.
Sometimes, we want to get others in trouble.

Send us your Spirit, Jesus,
to take the meanness
out of our hearts,
and to put kindness there instead.

Amen.

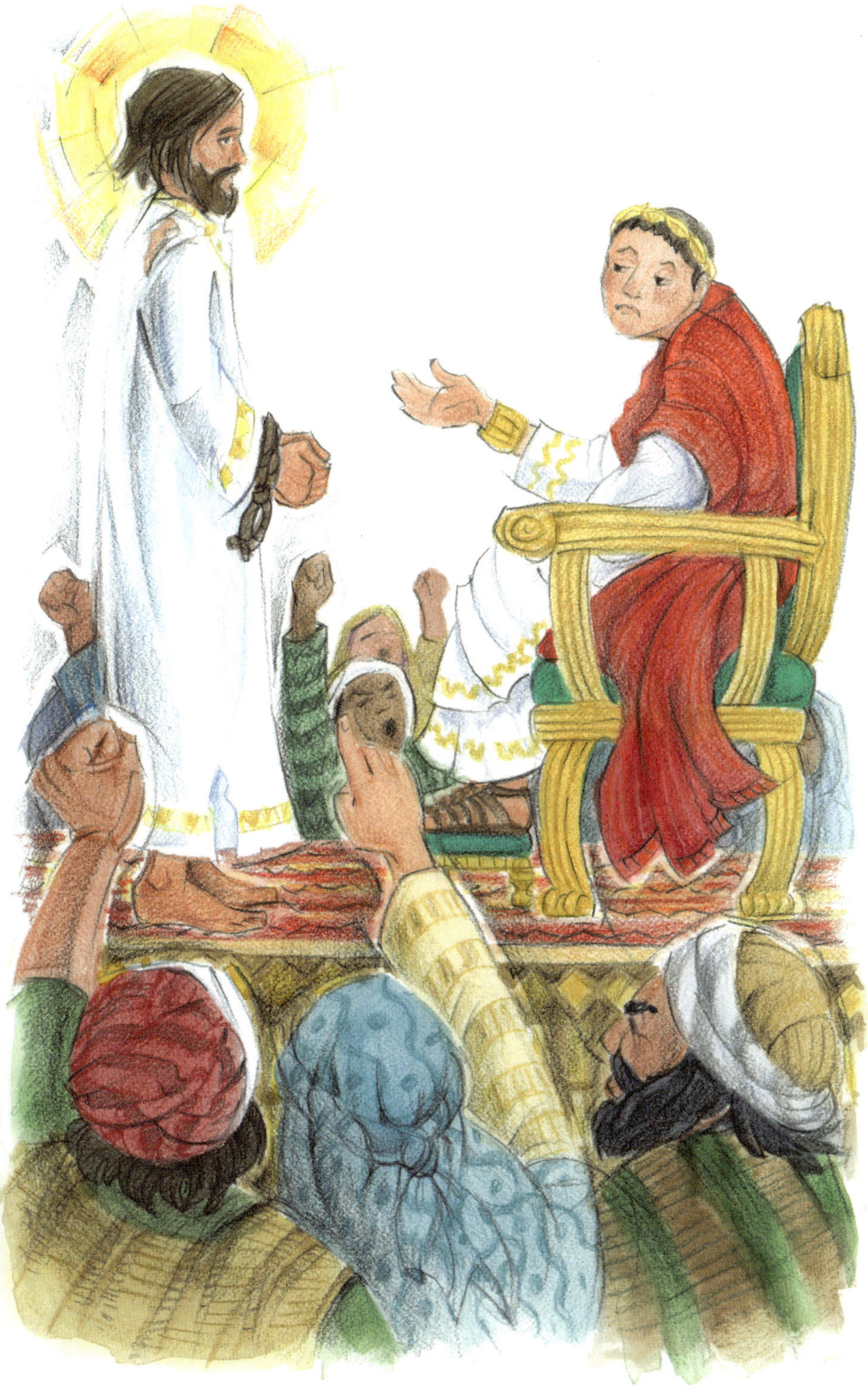

4
Jesus is scourged and crowned with thorns

Matthew 27:27-31

The soldiers made fun of Jesus.
They dressed him up as a king.
But instead of a real crown,
they put a crown of thorns on his head.
The thorns were sharp like needles.
The soldiers said mean words to Jesus,
and hit him until he started bleeding.

Let's be quiet with Jesus.

Let's pray.

Jesus, sometimes we feel
like we want to hurt someone
with our words or with our hands.
Don't let us do it!

Help us remember that when
we hurt someone
with our words or with our hands,
we hurt you, too.

Amen.

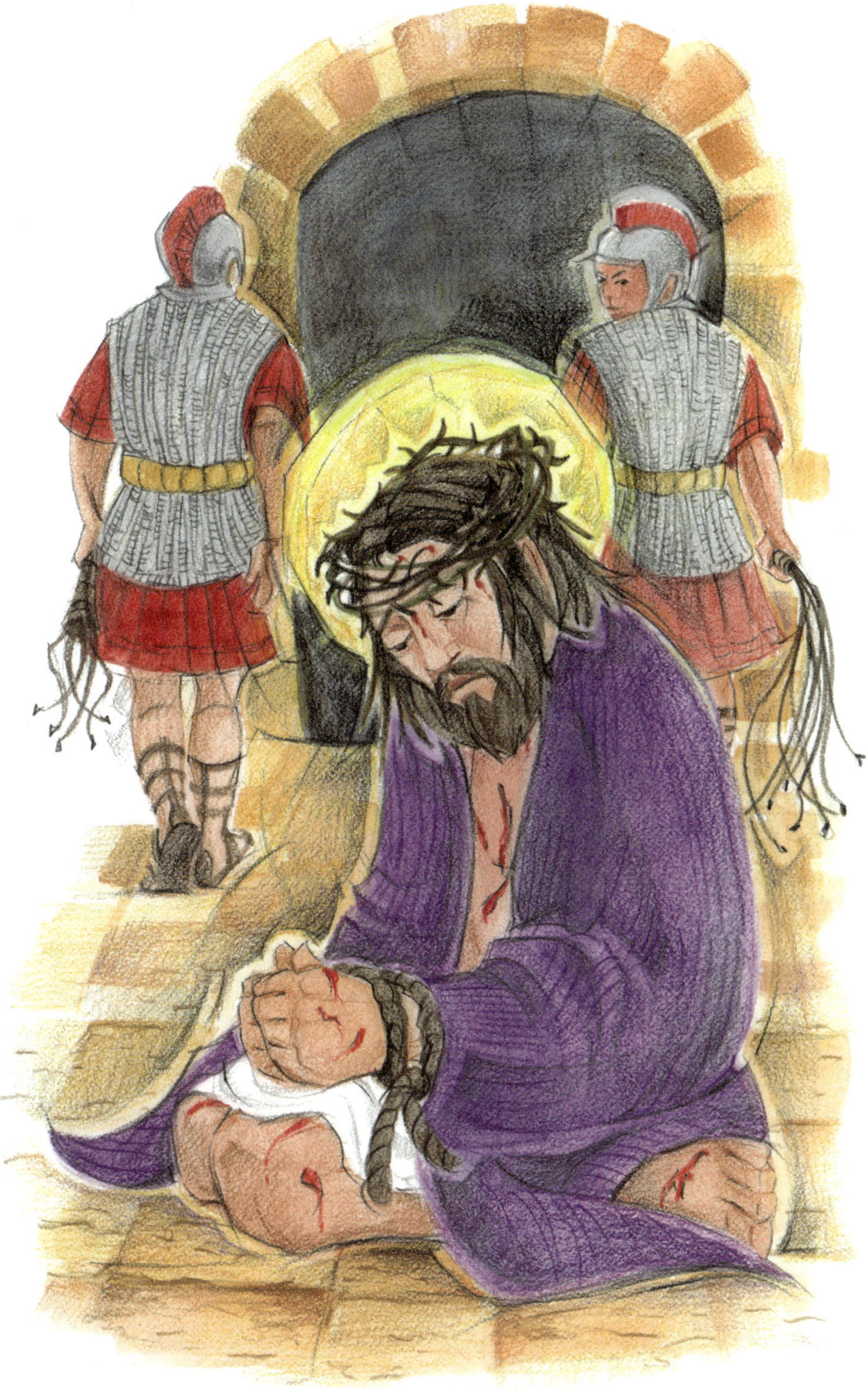

5
Jesus carries the cross
John 19:16-17

The soldiers made Jesus carry
a heavy wooden cross
all the way to a hill outside Jerusalem.
Some of his friends watched Jesus go,
and followed him along the way.

Let's be quiet with Jesus.

Let's pray.

Jesus, sometimes it is very hard
to follow your way,
especially when we feel
we are doing it alone.

Send your Spirit
to let us know
that we are never truly alone.
You are always with us,
ready to help.

Amen.

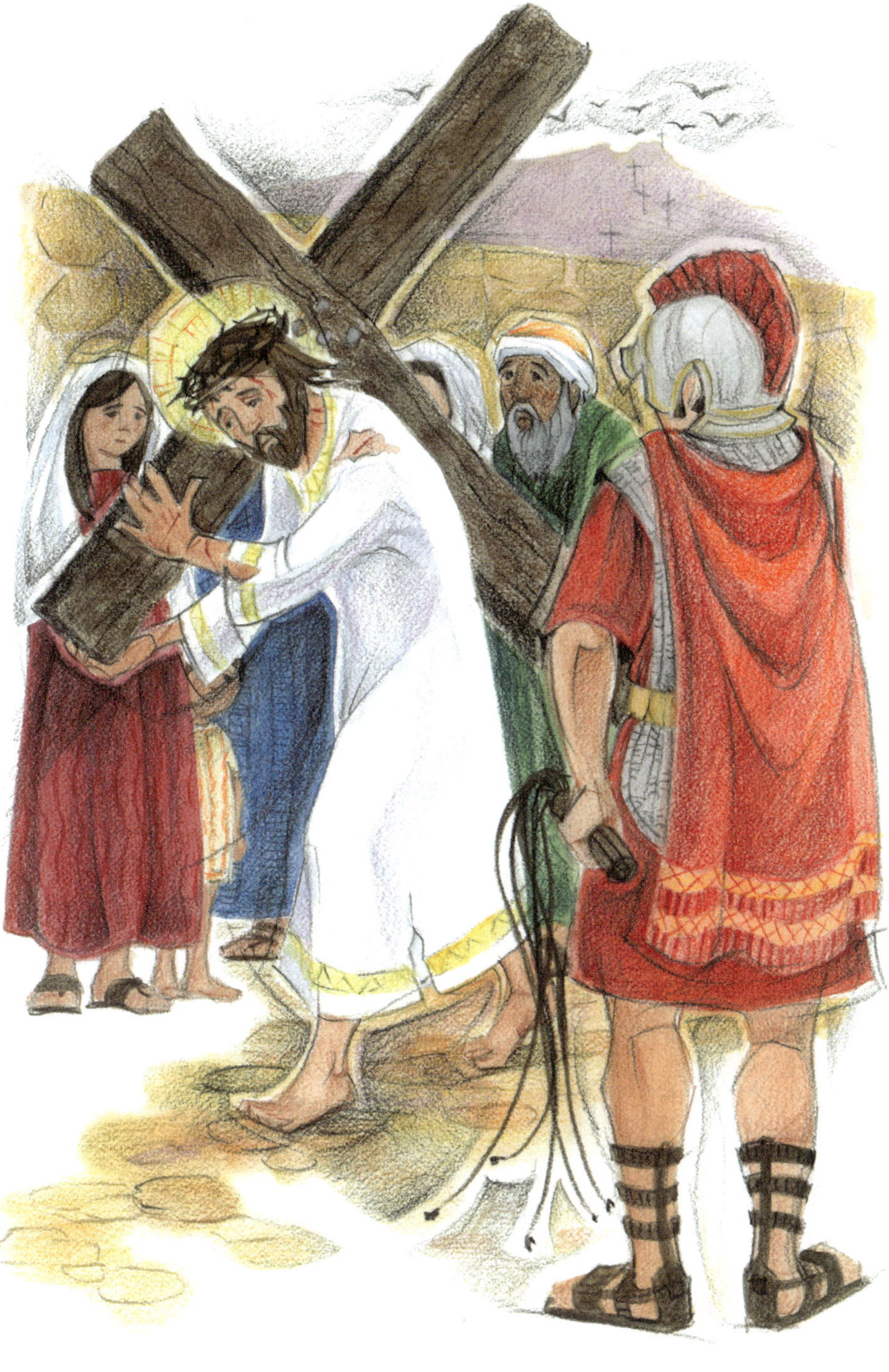

6
Jesus falls
Isaiah 53:4-7

When the cross
became too heavy to carry,
Jesus fell.
He could not rest,
because the soldiers made him
get up and keep going.

Let's be quiet with Jesus.

Let's pray.

Jesus, even though
you are the Son of God,
you took the weight of all our sins
onto yourself,
so that our sins would not
drag us down anymore.

Thank you, Jesus,
for carrying the cross
and saving us from sin.

Amen.

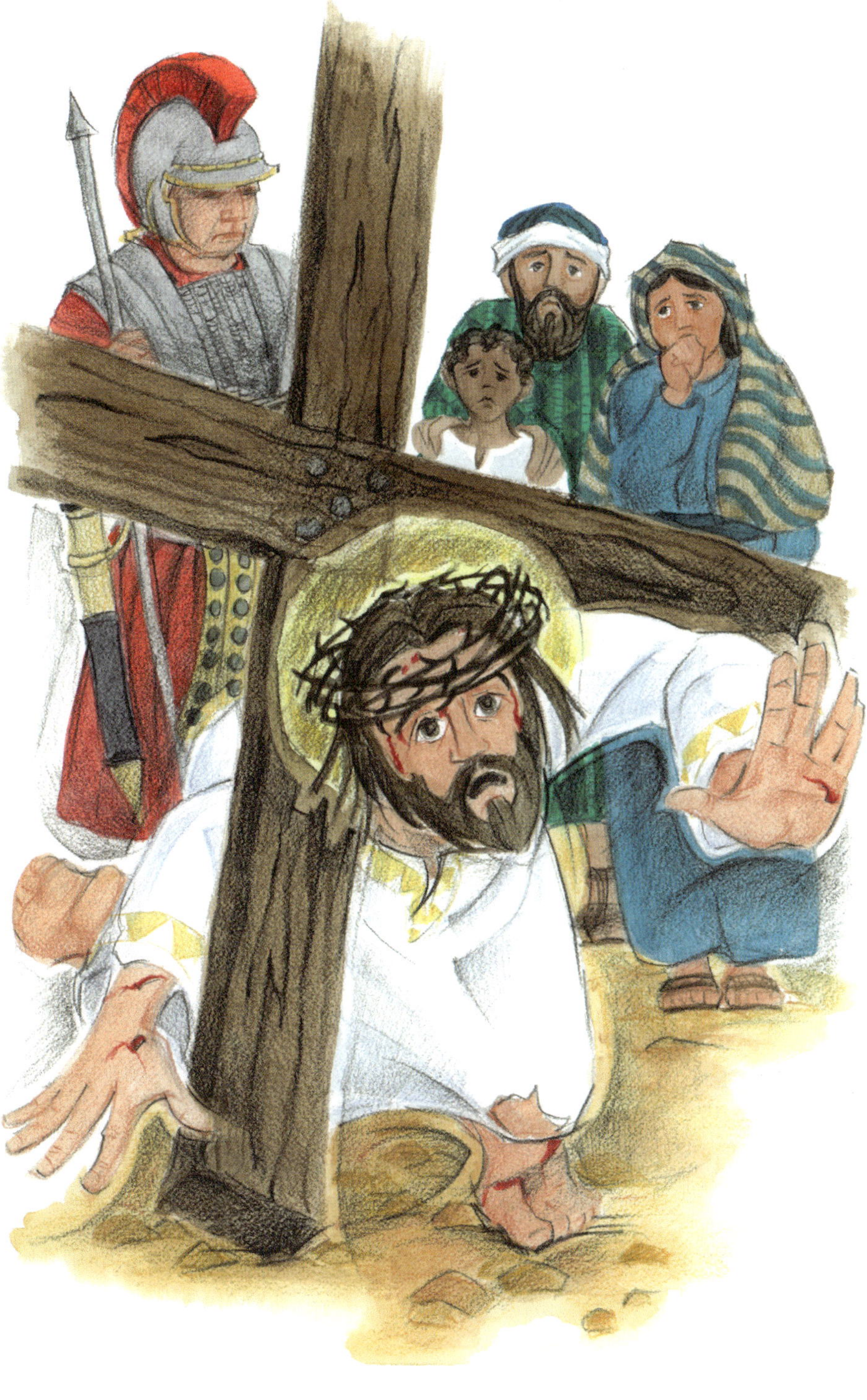

7
Simon of Cyrene helps Jesus carry the cross

Luke 23:26

When Jesus could no longer
carry the cross by himself,
a man named Simon
helped him carry it.

Let's be quiet with Jesus.

Let's pray.

Jesus, we want to help
carry your cross, too!
Show us how to help others,
especially those
who have too much to carry
by themselves.

Amen.

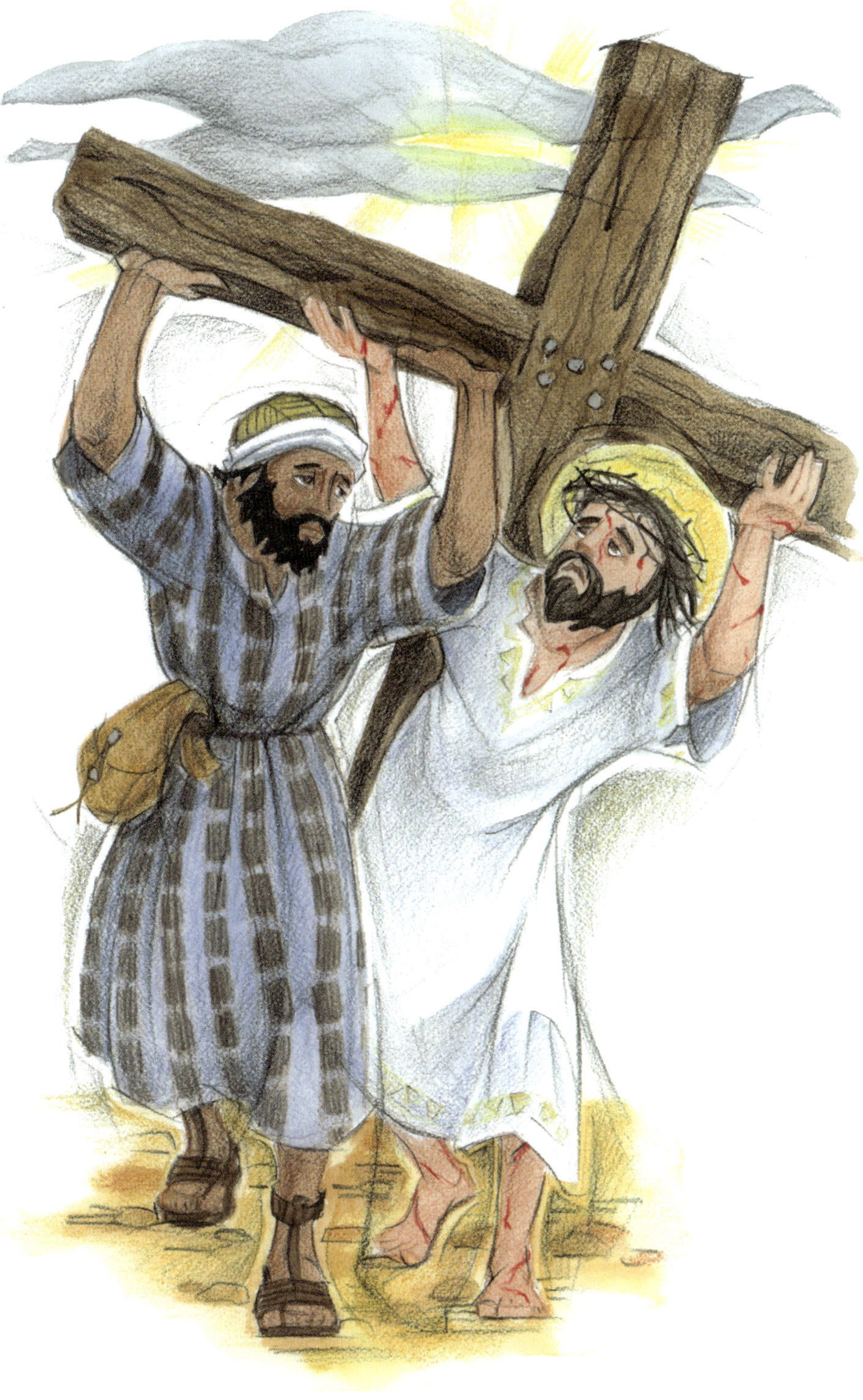

8
Jesus meets the women of Jerusalem

Luke 23:27–31

The women who followed Jesus
were crying because he was suffering.
Jesus talked to them,
and told them not to cry for him.

Let's be quiet with Jesus.

Let's pray.

Jesus, when we cry,
send your Spirit of peace
to comfort us.

When we see others crying,
give us words to comfort them.

Amen.

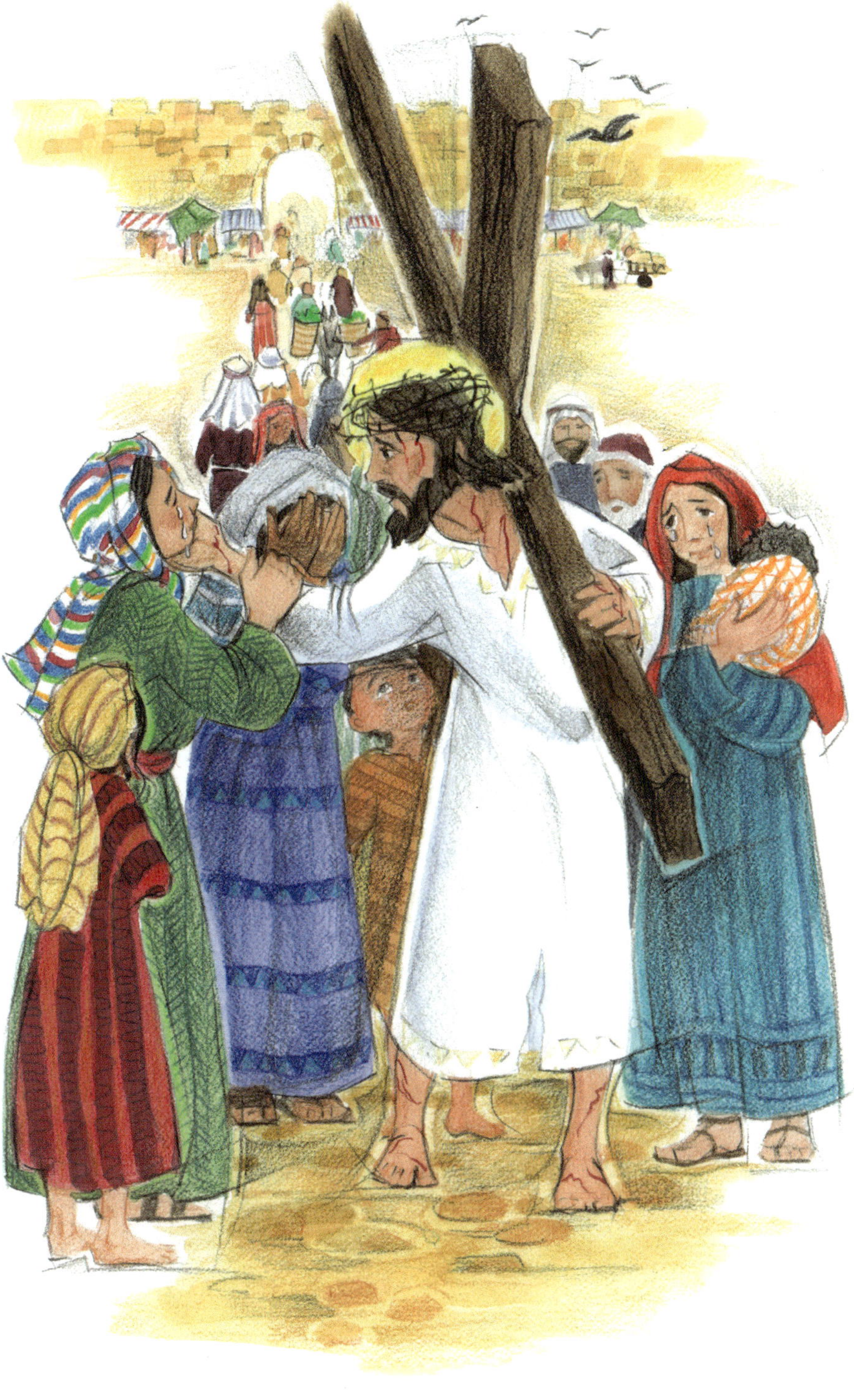

9
Jesus is nailed to the cross
Luke 23:32–38

When Jesus reached
a place called Golgotha,
the soldiers put nails
in his hands and in his feet,
and raised him up on the cross.
They put a sign above Jesus
that said, "King of the Jews."

Jesus said, "Father, forgive them,
because they do not know
what they are doing."

Let's be quiet with Jesus.

Let's pray.

Jesus, we're sorry
for the times we hurt you
by doing something wrong.

Thank you for loving us
even when we forget
to show our love for you!

Amen.

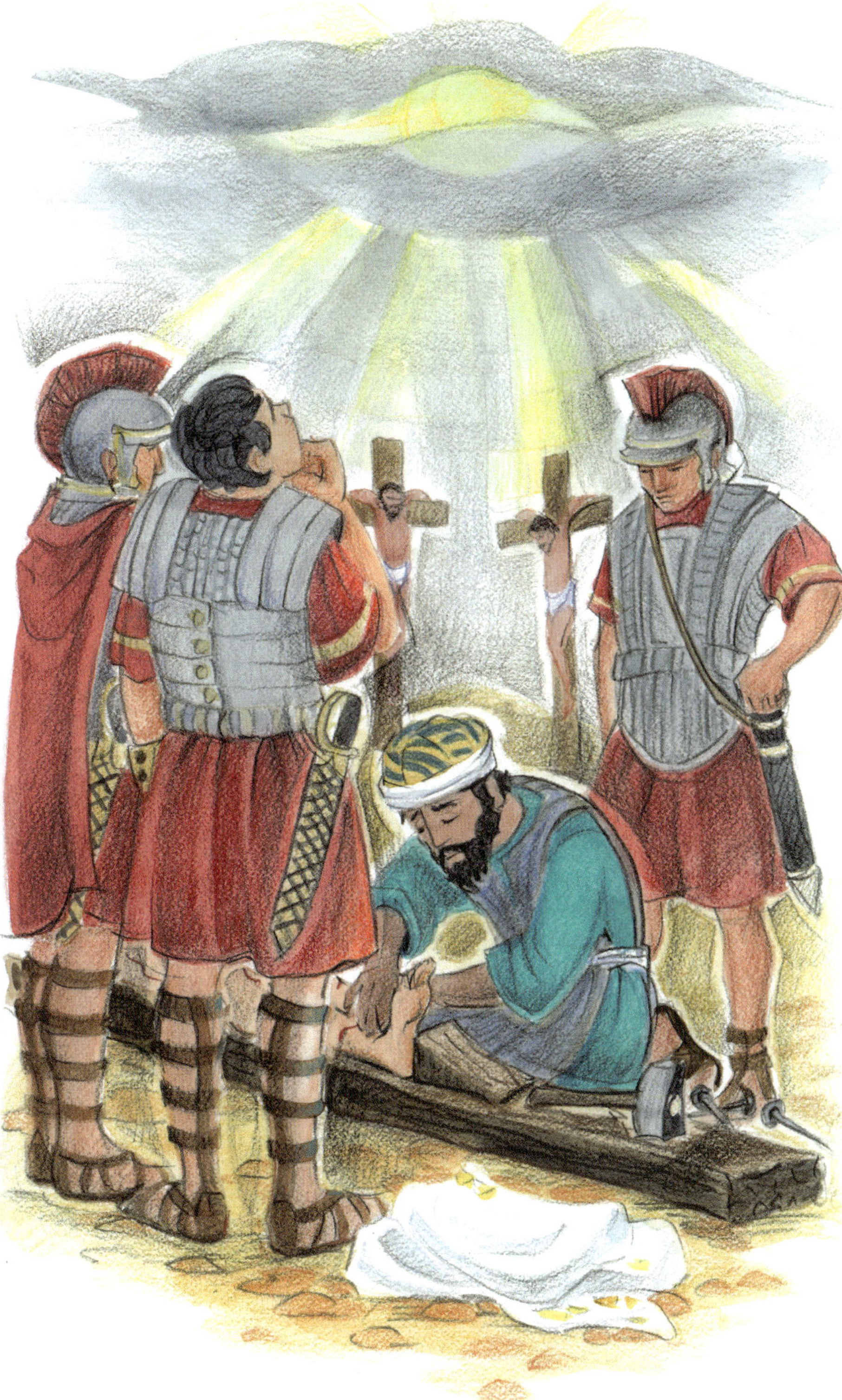

10
The Good Thief
Luke 23:39–43

Two men were crucified with Jesus.
They were being punished
for bad things they had done.
One man mocked Jesus,
but the other told him to stop.
He asked Jesus to take him to heaven,
and Jesus said he would.

Let's be quiet with Jesus.

Let's pray.

Jesus, we want to be with you, too,
both now and in heaven,
along with all our family and friends.

Help us to be like the Good Thief.
Help us say we are sorry for our sins,
and turn back to you.

Amen.

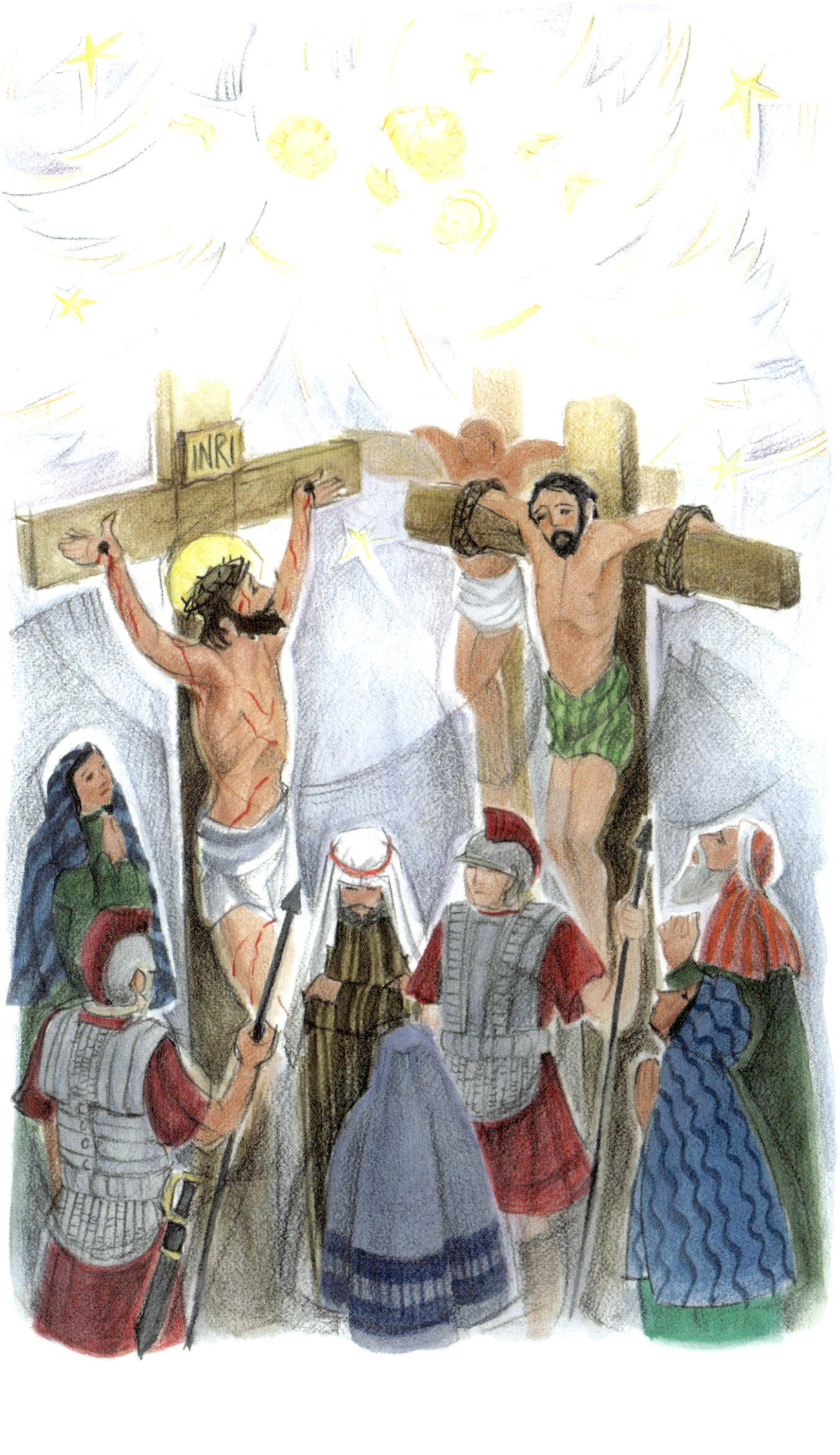
INRI

11
Mary and John at the foot of the cross

John 19:25–27

Mary, the mother of Jesus,
and John, one of the friends of Jesus,
were standing by the cross.
Jesus said to his mother,
"Here is your son."
He said to John,
"Here is your mother."

Let's be quiet with Jesus.

Let's pray.

Jesus, you gave your mother
not only to John,
but to everyone in the Church.
May your mother show us
her care and protection,
and lead us closer to you.

Amen.

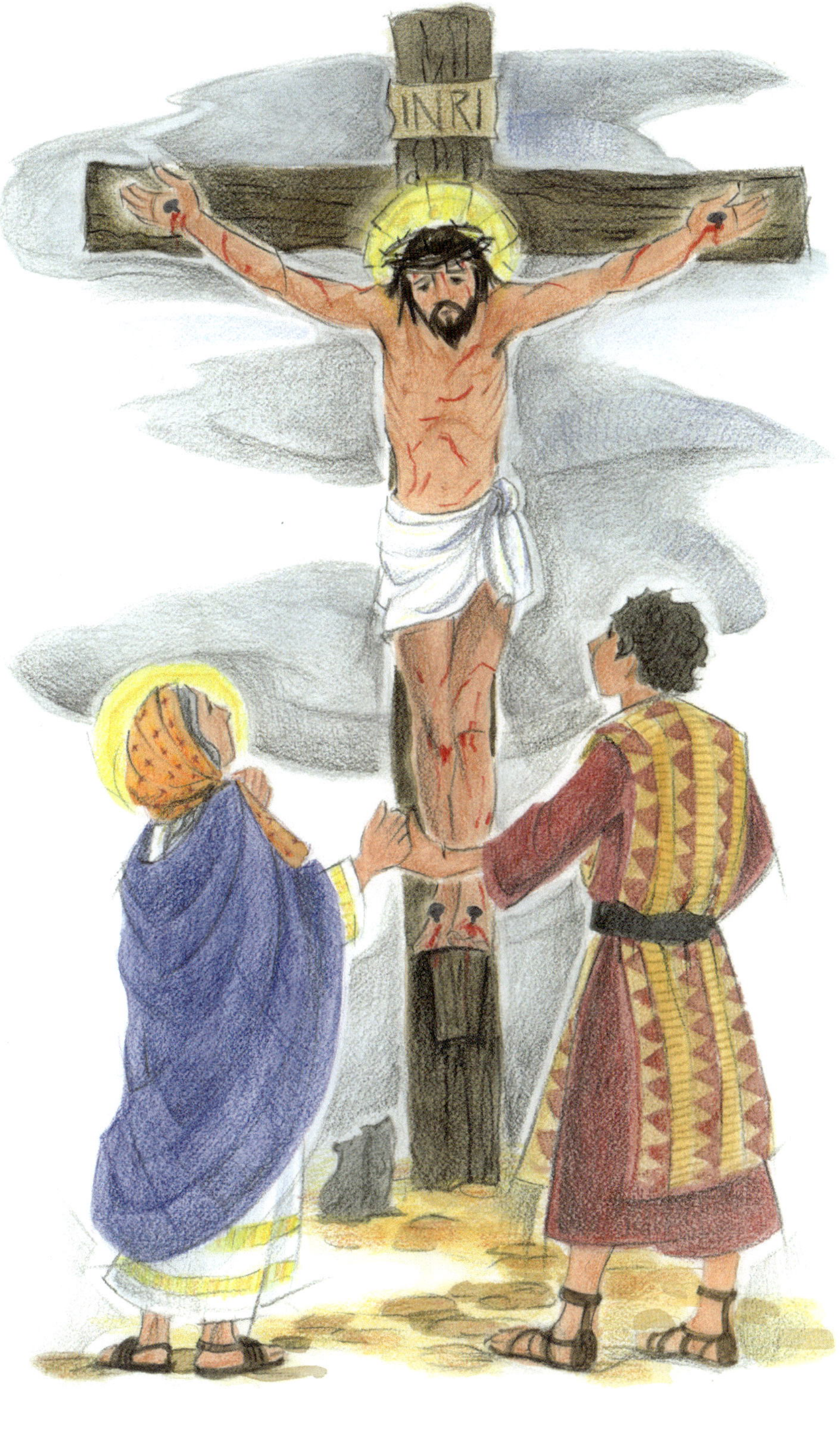
INRI

12
Jesus dies on the cross
John 19:28-30

Jesus said, "I thirst,"
so someone gave him
a little bit of wine to drink.
Then he said,
"It is finished," and died.

*Let's bow our heads or kneel
as we are quiet with Jesus.*

Let's pray.

Jesus, you are the Son of God,
the eternal Word
from the very beginning,
even before the stars.
But when we fell into sin,
you did not leave us to die.
In your love for us,
you came to rescue us
by taking our sins onto yourself.

We praise you, Jesus,
because by your holy cross,
you saved the whole world.

Amen.

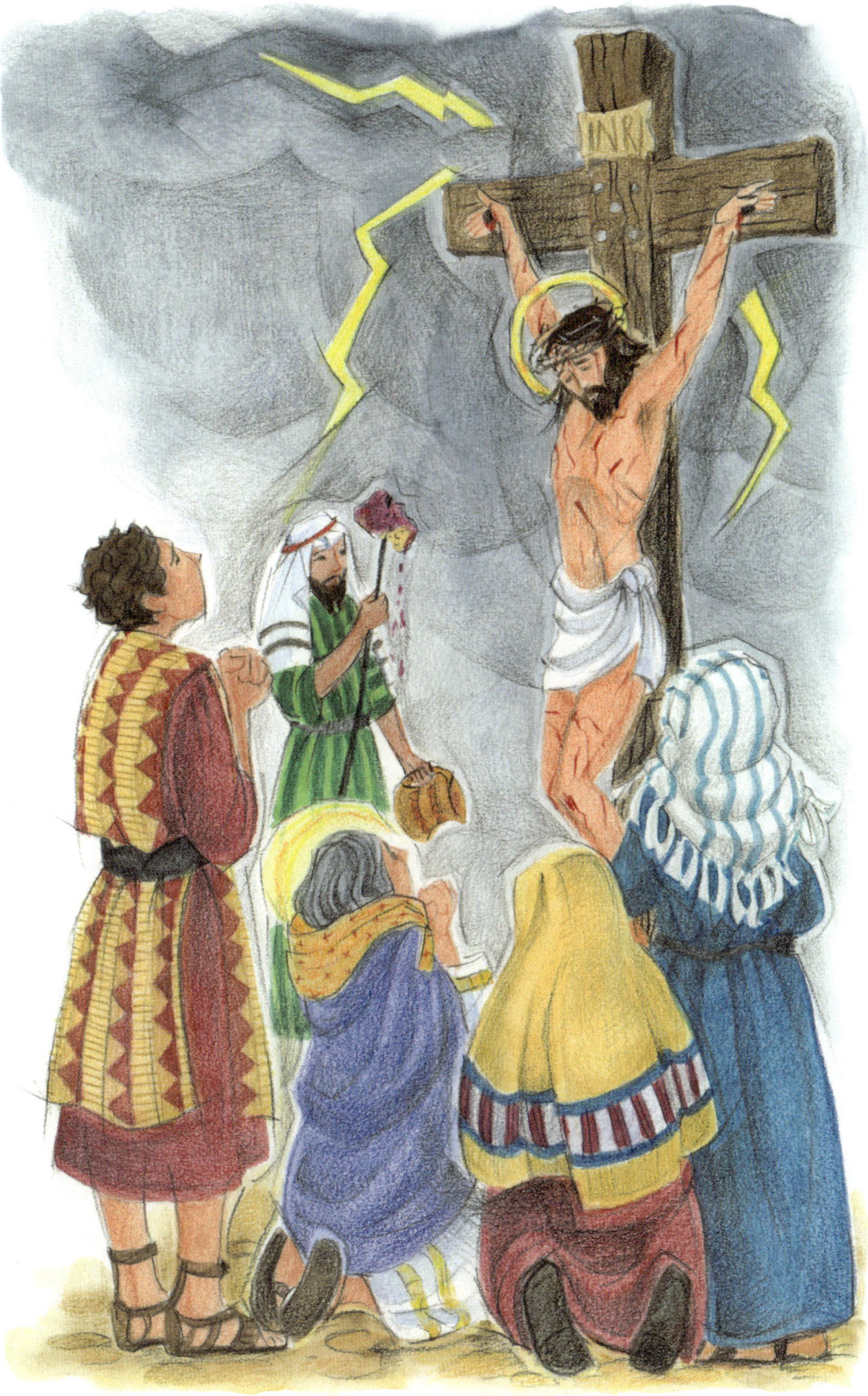
INRI

13
Jesus is laid in the tomb
John 19:38-42

After Jesus died,
his friends took his body
down from the cross.
They wrapped it in burial cloths
and placed it in a tomb.
Then they shut the tomb
with a large stone.

Let's be quiet with Jesus.

Let's pray.

Jesus, send your peace
to everyone who is sad
because someone they loved
has died.

And send your angels
to lead all those who have died
to the happiness of heaven.

Amen.

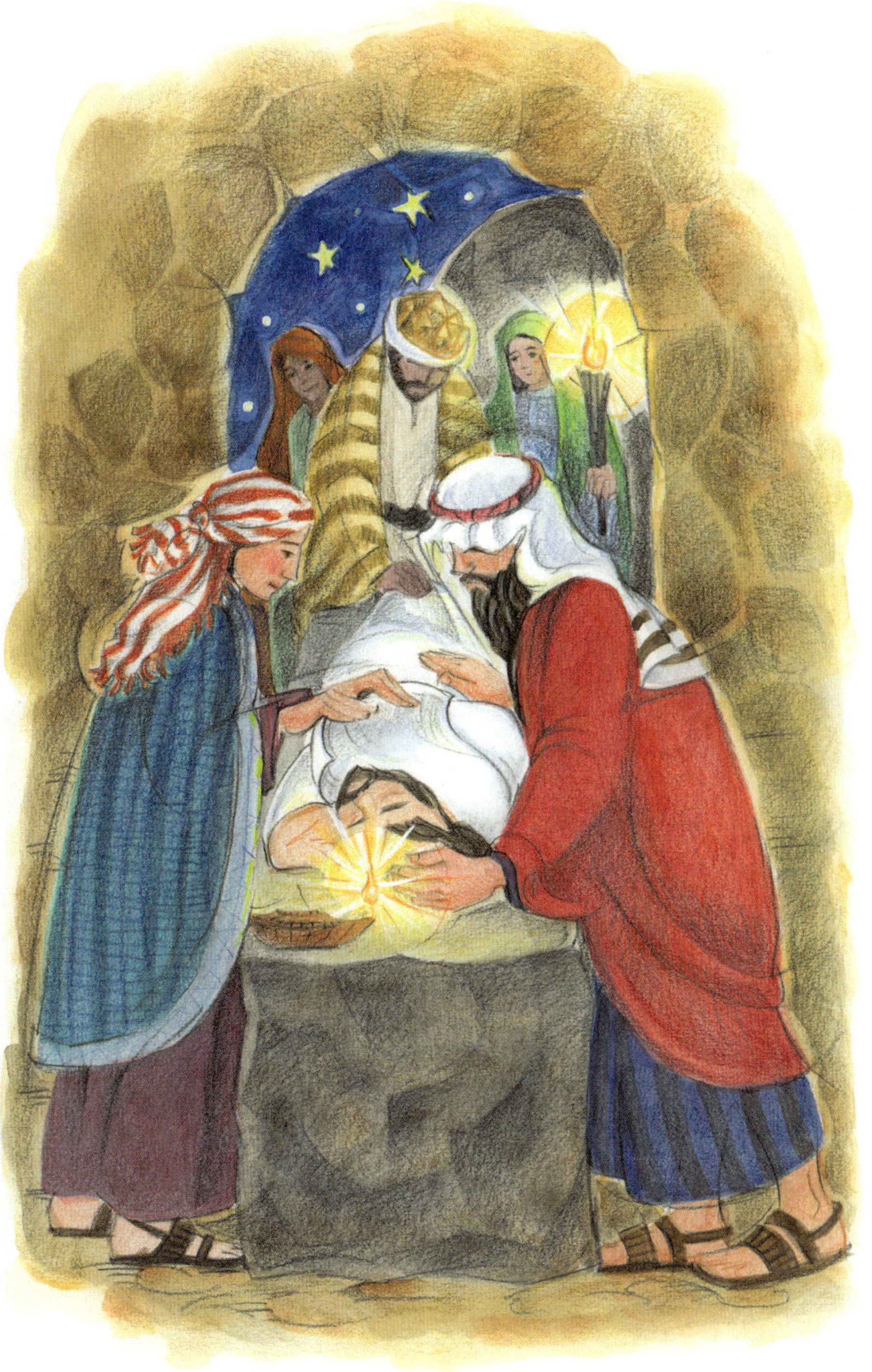

14
Jesus rises from the dead
Matthew 28:1-10

On Sunday morning,
some women visited the tomb
where Jesus' body had been laid.
But they did not find him there—
the tomb was empty!
An angel said to them,
"Do not be afraid;
Jesus is raised from the dead,
and you will see him soon."

Let's be quiet with Jesus.

Let's pray.

Jesus, you promised
that all who follow you
would be freed from sin and death.
Send your Spirit to help us follow you,
so that one day,
we may see your face
and live with you forever
in the joy and happiness of heaven.
Amen.

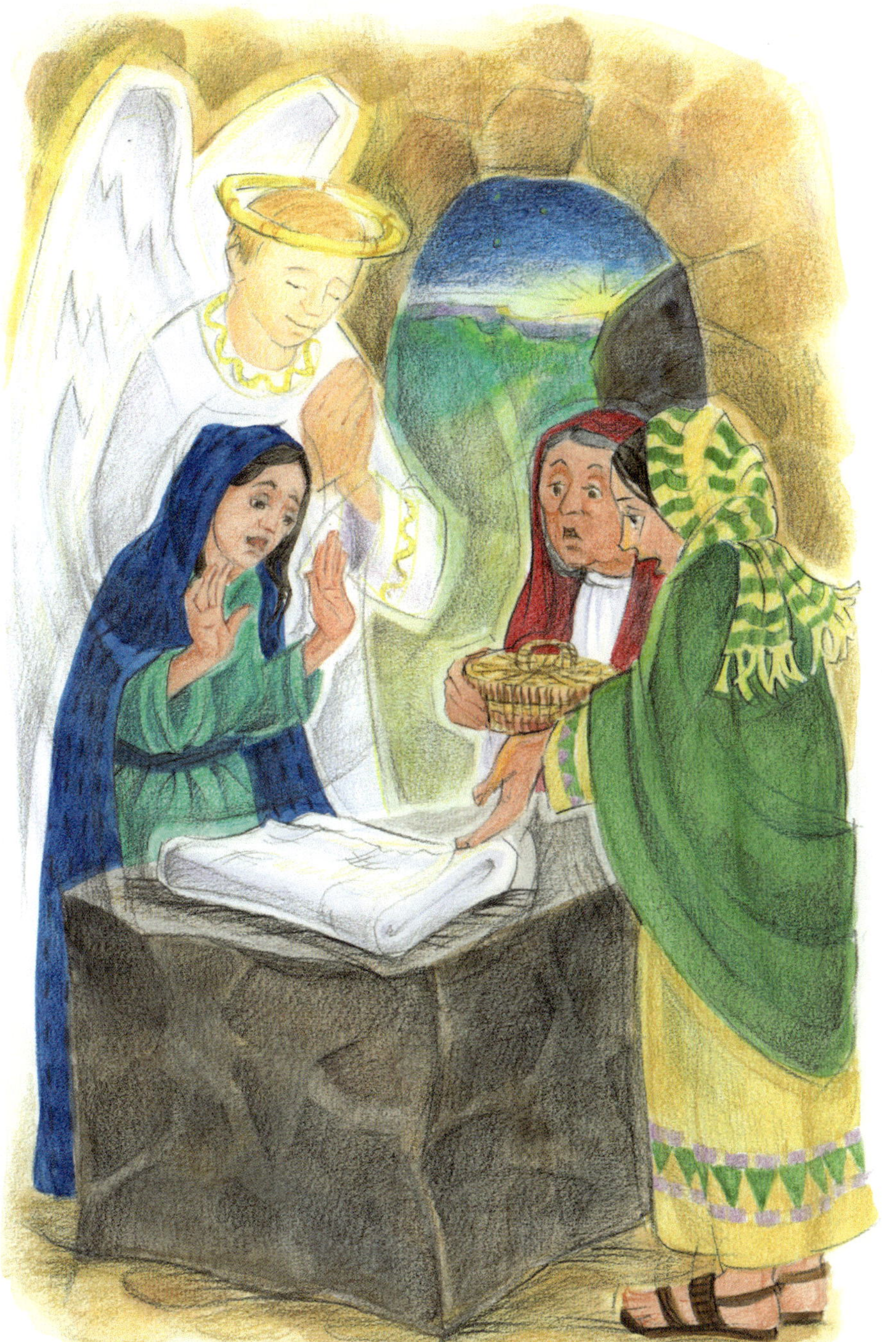

Closing Prayer

After Jesus rose from the dead,
he appeared to his friends.
His friends talked to him,
and touched him,
and ate food with him.
When the time came for Jesus
to return to his Father in heaven,
he did not leave his friends alone.
He sent them his Spirit
to help them continue
his work in the world.
Through his Spirit,
Jesus is with us today:
in his Church, in the sacraments,
and in his people.

Let's pray.

Jesus, you asked us to tell everyone
the Good News of your Resurrection.

Send your Spirit to help us
as we go out into the world,
following your Way
in all we do and say.

✝ **In the name of the Father, and of the Son, and of the Holy Spirit. Amen.**

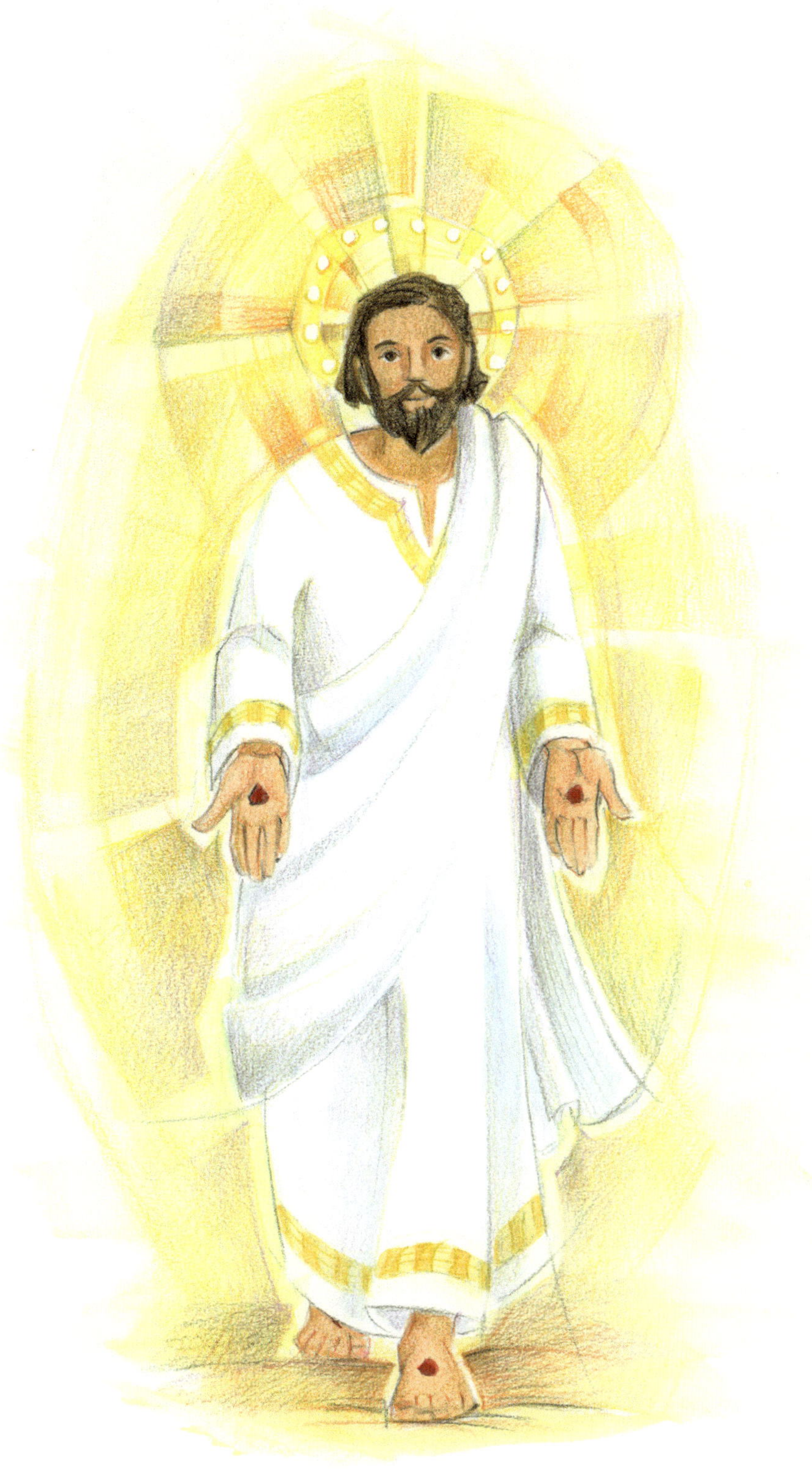

About This Book

Since the earliest centuries of the Church, Christians have made pilgrimages to Jerusalem in order to retrace the steps of Jesus during his suffering and death. Around the fifteenth century, Christians began the practice of prayerfully meditating on the Passion of Christ by reproducing that pilgrimage in miniature in what eventually became known as the Stations of the Cross.

Over the centuries, the Stations of the Cross have taken many forms. The form used in this book is the "New Way of the Cross" approved by the bishops of the Philippines and widely used there. It is well suited for younger children who are not yet familiar with the story of Jesus' Passion. It connects the sacrifice on Calvary to the sacrifice of the Mass, and it places that sacrifice within the larger context of the story of salvation. It also prepares children for the Triduum, which begins with our recollection of the Last Supper on Holy Thursday and ends with the Resurrection at the Easter Vigil.

Ways to Use This Book

Review these stations before using them with your children, noting where it would be good to adjust wording.

These stations are short and sweet, geared to the attention span of younger children. Encourage children to use the illustrations to help them meditate during the period of silence. Maintain the silence long enough to allow God to speak to your children. Thirty seconds is a reasonable goal for older children. For tips on using thirty seconds of silence with children, look up "Thirty Seconds of Silence" on the Peanut Butter & Grace website (pbgrace.com).

Here are some options for adapting these stations:

- Assign children who are able to read to lead each station, or a different part of each station.

- You or an older child may read the Scripture reference for each station from a Bible.

- Say or sing one or more of the optional prayers (page 35) before or after each station.

- With preschoolers, rather than reading the text, use it as a guide for having a conversation about the picture for each station.

- Posters of the illustrations in this book are available from Gracewatch Media. Consider using these to make a Way of the Cross in your home or church.

Optional Prayers

Stabat Mater Dolorosa
At the cross her station keeping,
stood the mournful mother weeping,
close to Jesus to the last.
Through her heart, his sorrow sharing,
all his bitter anguish bearing,
now at length the sword had passed.

We Adore You
We adore you, O Christ, and we praise you,
because by your holy cross, you have redeemed the world.

Our Father
Our Father
who art in heaven,
hallowed be thy name;
thy kingdom come;
thy will be done
on earth as it is in heaven.
Give us this day our daily bread;
and forgive us our trespasses
as we forgive those who trespass against us;
and lead us not into temptation,
but deliver us from evil.
Amen.

Printed in Great Britain
by Amazon